CW01150451

Original title:
Moonbeams and Night Songs

Copyright © 2024 Creative Arts Management OÜ
All rights reserved.

Author: Cassandra Whitaker
ISBN HARDBACK: 978-9916-90-686-6
ISBN PAPERBACK: 978-9916-90-687-3

Nighttime Reveries and Silver Glints

In the hush of night so deep,
Dreams awaken from their sleep.
Whispers float on moonlit air,
Silver glints adorn the fair.

Stars above like scattered seeds,
Telling tales of ancient deeds.
Glimmers dance on velvet skies,
Filling hearts with softest sighs.

A silent world where shadows play,
Guiding thoughts that drift away.
In this realm of quiet grace,
Time suspends in love's embrace.

Flickering Lights in the Stillness

Flickering lights in the calm of night,
Casting soft shadows, a gentle sight.
Each glow a story, each beam a thought,
In the stillness, dreams are caught.

The world outside fades to gray,
Inside, warm sparks invite us to stay.
With every pulse, the silence sings,
Of hopeful tomorrows and fragile things.

Between breaths, the moments sway,
Guiding hearts in a tender ballet.
In the dark, we find our way,
As flickering lights gently play.

Enchantment of the Quiet Hours

In quiet hours, magic brews,
Where peace whispers and stars choose.
The night unfolds with gentle grace,
Enchanting hearts in its warm embrace.

Dreams cascade like soft silver streams,
Weaving together our deepest dreams.
In the silence, wisdom thrives,
As the soul awakens, love survives.

Time slows down, the world aside,
In this haven, we can confide.
Each moment lingers, a cherished pearl,
In the enchantment of this world.

Harmonies Written in Starlight

Harmonies play in the midnight air,
Written softly, beyond compare.
Notes like jewels, they softly weave,
Melodies born in the night's reprieve.

Stars align, a celestial choir,
Lifting spirits, sparking desire.
Every twinkle tells a tale,
Of lovers, dreamers, a moonlit trail.

With every breath, the night transforms,
In the dark, creativity warms.
Together, let's dance in this light,
To harmonies written in starlight.

Whispers of Silver Light

In the hush of night so bright,
Moonbeams dance, a gentle sight.
Softly whispered winds so clear,
Carrying dreams for all to hear.

Shadows play in silver gleam,
Echoes of a tender dream.
Stars above in quiet flight,
Guide our hearts with pure delight.

Serenade of Celestial Dreams

Softly sings the evening star,
Cradling wishes from afar.
Galaxies in swirling grace,
Wrap us in their warm embrace.

Echoes of a cosmic tune,
Dancing neath the watchful moon.
Every heartbeat, every sigh,
Transports us into the sky.

Lullabies in the Starlit Sky

Songs of night, a sweet refrain,
Carried softly on the plain.
Starlit whispers, soft and low,
Guide us where our dreams can flow.

Cradled in the arms of night,
Wrapped in love, a pure delight.
Sleep now, let your spirit soar,
In the sky, forevermore.

Radiance Beneath the Twilight Canopy

Beneath the sky of painted hues,
Twilight wraps the world in blues.
Fading light begins to play,
Melodies of closing day.

Whispers of the night unfold,
Secrets of the dusk retold.
In the glow of soft retreat,
Heartbeats echo, steady beat.

Cosmic Hues and Whispered Dreams

In the vast expanse we wander,
Stars like jewels in a sea of night.
Dreams woven in cosmic splendor,
Softly shimmer, a guiding light.

Colors dance in celestial whirl,
Nebulas bloom with vibrant grace.
Whispers of fate in the universe's pearl,
Each heartbeat feels the timeless chase.

Galaxies spin, a wondrous show,
The fabric of time, a silken thread.
In the silence, our spirits flow,
To the rhythm of the stars, we're led.

Together we chase the twilight glow,
In the depths of the endless sky.
Where the heart knows, the soul will go,
In cosmic hues, forever fly.

The Glow of Hopes in the Dark

When shadows creep and silence hums,
A flicker rises from within.
In the stillness, a heartbeat drums,
Hope ignites, a spark to spin.

Through the night, the whispers sway,
Guiding dreams with tender light.
Amidst the gloom, we find our way,
Embers flicker, brave the night.

Challenges rise, and fears take flight,
Yet we stand firm, unyielding friends.
With each step, we claim our right,
For in our hearts, the light transcends.

In the darkest hour, we are found,
Holding tight to what we believe.
The glow of hopes, a sacred sound,
In unity, we shall achieve.

Fragments of Light Amidst Shadows

Shadows stretch, as daylight wanes,
Yet fragments shimmer, pierce the dark.
In hidden corners, joy remains,
Guided by each tender spark.

In the quiet, a chorus sings,
Echoing hope through time and space.
Life's beauty lies in simple things,
In every shadow, find your grace.

Moments shared beneath the veil,
Laughter mingles with the tears.
Every story, a timeless tale,
Weaving light through all our fears.

So let us dance, our spirits free,
Amidst the shadows, we create.
For every fragment, a memory,
Illuminates our shared fate.

Luminous Secrets of the Starlit Quiet

Beneath the stars, in tranquil nights,
Secrets linger in the air.
Whispers carry in gentle flights,
A cosmic dance, a sacred prayer.

Every twinkle holds a promise,
Of dreams that shimmer in the vast.
In the quiet, life's sweet bliss,
Memories etched, forever cast.

We gather round, beneath the glow,
Voices soft as twilight's sigh.
In starlit quiet, time flows slow,
As hearts unite beneath the sky.

So let the darkness softly cradle,
The luminous tales we weave and spin.
In whispered truths, we find our fable,
As starlit secrets, shine within.

Nocturnal Serenade of the Heart

In shadows deep, our whispers flow,
Beneath the stars, where soft winds blow.
The night wears silk, a velvet shroud,
Embracing dreams, both sweet and loud.

Moonlit paths, we wander slow,
With every breath, the soft aglow.
In silence shared, our souls unite,
A serenade, pure and bright.

Gleaming Melodies in Darkened Dreams

Melodies rise from twilight's veil,
Echoing hearts, they sail and sail.
Notes of longing, weaving tight,
In the silence, pure delight.

Through veils of mist, the music plays,
Dancing shadows, a soft ballet.
In dreams we find our secret song,
In darkened nights where we belong.

Soft Hues of the Dusk

The sun dips low, a painter's hand,
Brushes the sky with colors grand.
Soft hues blend, a gentle sigh,
As day gives way to night's sweet cry.

Whispers float on twilight's breath,
Life and dreams, an artful bequeath.
In dusk's embrace, the world will pause,
For in this glow, we find our cause.

Echoes of Secrets in the Moonlight

Echoes dance on silver beams,
Unveiling hearts, revealing dreams.
In moonlit realms, where shadows play,
Secrets unfold, come what may.

A tapestry of stars above,
We share our fears, our hopes, our love.
In whispers soft, the night will hear,
As the moon glows bright, and draws us near.

Hushed Melodies of the Darkened Wood

In shadows deep, where whispers dwell,
The secrets of the night do swell.
The leaves converse in gentle sighs,
As moonlight dances, softly flies.

A rustling sound, a timid deer,
Its heartbeat kept, the world so near.
The branches creak, the owls do call,
In this embrace, we share it all.

With every step, the silence blooms,
The forest sings, dispelling glooms.
Beneath the stars, where dreams align,
The wood reveals a magic divine.

Together we commune with grace,
Lost in the night, this timeless space.
As hush descends, the world succumbs,
To melodies that nature hums.

Ethereal Glow of the Midnight Hour

The clock strikes twelve, a glow ignites,
Illuminating mysterious sights.
A silver veil drapes the night sky,
As dreams unravel and fates comply.

Beneath the stars, the world stands still,
Time melds with air, a gentle thrill.
Soft whispers weave through velvet air,
A promise held in midnight's glare.

The moon, a guardian, shines so bright,
Bathing the earth in soft twilight.
Each shadow dances, each secret breath,
In this hour, we defy death.

Ethereal glimpses, moments rare,
We wander through this enchanted layer.
Time bends, and hearts enclose,
In the glow where the magic flows.

Echoes of the Dusk's Embrace

As daylight fades, a hush descends,
The sun retreats, the night intends.
With colors soft, the twilight spreads,
As stars awaken from their beds.

The echoes call from hills afar,
A serenade by the evening star.
The world transforms in dusky hue,
A delicate blend of red and blue.

With every breath, the magic swells,
In nature's arms, the heart compels.
As shadows lengthen, dreams arise,
In dusk's embrace, the spirit flies.

Together lost in moments rare,
We chase the night, without a care.
The echoes linger, secrets keep,
In twilight's hold, we softly sleep.

Chasing Shadows in the Nocturnal Breeze

In midnight's clutch, we chase the shadows,
Through quiet paths where the cool wind blows.
A labyrinth of whispers in every tree,
Guides our footsteps, wild and free.

The moonlight plays, a game of hide,
While restless spirits wander beside.
With every gust, a tale unfolds,
Of ancient nights and stories told.

We dance to rhythms only felt,
In hushed tones, our dreams are dealt.
The shadows stretch, they beckon near,
In this embrace, we shed our fear.

With hearts aflame and eyes that gleam,
We chase the night, we live the dream.
In every breath, in every sigh,
The nocturnal breeze will never die.

Sonnet of the Evening's Breath

The sun descends, a golden hue,
While shadows stretch, the day bids adieu.
Soft breezes play through trees aligned,
A tranquil peace, in dusk we find.

Stars awaken, twinkling bright,
Whispers of dreams dance in the night.
Moonlight bathes the world in grace,
The evening's breath, a soft embrace.

Nocturnal Blossoms and Gentle Whispers

In gardens where the night unfolds,
Nocturnal blooms, their story told.
Petals glisten, kissed by dew,
A symphony of shades and hue.

The wind carries whispers low,
Secrets only shadows know.
Crickets serenade the dark,
A melody, a gentle spark.

The Silvery Tryst of Nightfall

When twilight wraps the world in silk,
Stars emerge, their glow like milk.
The horizon dons a cloak of blue,
As night reveals its tranquil view.

With silvery beams, the moon shall rise,
Casting dreams across the skies.
In this meeting, souls convene,
Whispers shared, unseen, serene.

Reverie Beneath the Cosmic Veil

Beneath the cosmos, vast and deep,
We find the dreams that night will keep.
Galaxies swirl in silent flight,
As hearts entwine in soft twilight.

Wishes fly on stardust trails,
Each heartbeat echoes, love prevails.
In reverie, we find our way,
Guided by the night's ballet.

Reflections Under an Indigo Canopy

Beneath a sky of deepening hue,
Whispers of dreams begin to stir.
Leaves dance to a secret tune,
Nature's heart begins to purr.

Rivers mirror the twilight glow,
Painting stories on the surface.
Each ripple tells what we don't know,
Time steps back, it's all so vast.

Stars awaken in silent grace,
Adorning night with silver threads.
In this tranquil, sacred space,
We find the peace that gently spreads.

A moment caught, eternity held,
In indigo, we breathe and sigh.
Here in the stillness, hearts are melded,
The night unfolds, and so do I.

Harmonics of the Star-Sprinkled Sky

Celestial music fills the night,
Notes of wonder linger still.
Constellations, pure delight,
Each twinkle, a captured thrill.

Lunar beams kiss the meadow's face,
In shadows, secrets softly creep.
Harmony guides the night's embrace,
As dreams emerge from restful sleep.

A breeze carries the tales of old,
Whispered wishes on the wind.
In starlight, our hearts unfold,
Transformation where dreams begin.

Together here, we share this space,
Under the sky, our spirits soar.
Each breath a promise, a gentle grace,
In harmonics, forevermore.

Twilight's Breath on Gentle Waters

Lakes reflect the evening's sigh,
As hues of amber softly blend.
The sun dips low, a fleeting high,
Nature's canvas begins to mend.

Ripples dance in tender light,
Kissing shores of tranquil land.
In twilight's glow, all feels right,
The world pauses to understand.

Shadows stretch with gentle hands,
Caressing moments filled with grace.
In silence, the heart expands,
As peace finds its rightful place.

Each breath is woven, soft and deep,
A lullaby for weary souls.
The waters cradle secrets we keep,
In twilight's arms, our spirits whole.

Soft Cadences of the Dreaming Night

In the hush of night, dreams unfurl,
Whispers carried on tender air.
Stars align, their stories swirl,
A symphony beyond compare.

Moonlight drapes the world in silver,
Illuminating paths we tread.
In soft shadows, heartbeats quiver,
Guided by what's left unsaid.

Each note sung by the crickets' hymn,
Resonates with the pulse of life.
In darkness, where hopes begin,
We embrace the calm, free from strife.

Close your eyes to the night's soft kiss,
Let its cadence cradle your mind.
In dreaming's warmth, find your bliss,
In sweet rhythms, peace you'll find.

A Dance with the Stars Above

Under the velvet sky so deep,
Stars twinkle as they start to leap.
Whispers of night embrace the air,
Moonlight casts shadows, soft and fair.

Dancing dreams drift on gentle breeze,
Each heartbeat syncs with rustling leaves.
Galaxies twirl in a cosmic waltz,
As we surrender to night's exalts.

We spin like comets, wild and free,
In the arms of starlight's harmony.
With every twirl, the world fades out,
In this embrace, there's no more doubt.

Sable Serenades and Glimmering Thoughts

In twilight's hush, a melody sings,
Sable shadows where mystery clings.
Thoughts like fireflies begin to glow,
Glimmering softly, a wondrous show.

Through tangled dreams, the siren calls,
Echoes of night in silken halls.
Serenades wrapped in starlit sighs,
As shadows dance beneath midnight skies.

Each whispered note, a tale untold,
Wrapped in silver, soft and bold.
Hearts flutter like wings in flight,
In sable serenades of the night.

The Allure of the Night's Gaze

In the stillness, the night unfolds,
Secrets held in its quiet holds.
Stars ignite in the depths of blue,
Every twinkle, a story anew.

The moon, a sentinel, watches near,
Casting its glow over all we hold dear.
In the allure of its gentle light,
Dreams arise, taking gentle flight.

Whispers of love float on the breeze,
Binding hearts with a timeless ease.
In the night's gaze, we find our place,
Lost in the magic, time we embrace.

Enchanted Rhythms of Stillness

In the stillness, the world holds its breath,
Time pauses, gripped in a gentle depth.
Rhythms echo in heartbeats near,
Every silence, a melody clear.

Nature weaves its hushed design,
Moonlight dances with shadows divine.
Stars align in a celestial grace,
Enchanted whispers fill the space.

Moments linger like softest sighs,
In the hush where true magic lies.
Wrapped in stillness, our spirits soar,
As we cherish what life has in store.

In the Embrace of Gentle Glimmers

In the twilight's soft caress,
Stars begin to softly bless.
Whispers of the night unfold,
Dreams of silver, tales of gold.

Moonlight dances on the stream,
Crickets sing a soft moonbeam.
Echoes linger, sweet and clear,
Nature's song is always near.

Branches sway with gentle grace,
Nighttime wears a calming face.
In the quiet, hearts align,
Finding solace, pure, divine.

As the world drifts into sleep,
Secrets in the shadows creep.
In this haven, time stands still,
In the glimmers, find your will.

The Language of the Silent Hours

When the sun bows down to rest,
Night unveils her languid quest.
Stars become a soothing balm,
In the dark, the world's at calm.

Each tick whispers tales untold,
In the hush, a spell unfolds.
Moments weave in silken threads,
Thoughts drift softly in our heads.

Shadows play a gentle game,
Flickering lights begin to tame.
In the silence, truth persists,
Echoes linger, can't resist.

Time stands still, the heart aligns,
In this peace, the spirit shines.
In the stillness, love's embrace,
Silent hours, a sacred space.

Silhouettes in the Dim Glow

Figures dance in twilight's hue,
Shadows cast in softest blue.
Whispers float on evening air,
In the dark, we lay our care.

Forms entwined in mellow light,
Holding dreams throughout the night.
Echoes of a laughter sweet,
Moments shared, a heartbeat's beat.

In the corners, secrets hide,
Cloaked in night, they gently bide.
Fingers trace the stars above,
In the dim glow, we find love.

As the night begins to fade,
Memories in silence laid.
Silhouettes in fading gleam,
Chasing softly every dream.

The Riddles of the Moonlit Realm

In the realm where shadows play,
Moonlight leads us through the gray.
Questions linger in the night,
Riddles whispered, out of sight.

Stars like gems in velvet skies,
Hidden truths in soft replies.
Hearts entwined with fate's own thread,
In the dark, our spirits wed.

Every twinkle holds a tale,
Stories shared without a trail.
In the hush, our secrets blend,
In this realm, there's no end.

Glimmers rise, like hopes reborn,
In the light of the new morn.
Riddles danced beneath the stars,
In the moonlit night's memoirs.

Night's Embrace, a Gentle Caress

In darkness deep, the stars do gleam,
Whispers float, like softest dream.
Moonlight dances, shadows play,
A hush that wraps the world in sway.

Gentle breeze through rustling trees,
Carrying secrets on the seas.
The nightingale sings low and clear,
In night's embrace, all sorrows sear.

Crickets chirp their night refrain,
Softly woven through the pain.
The air is thick with hopes and fears,
A gentle caress, the heart it steers.

With every breath, a lullaby,
Underneath the velvet sky.
In twilight's hold, we drift and sway,
Night's embrace leads us away.

Radiance Through the Shimmering Veil

Veils of silver, soft and bright,
Whisper dreams beneath the night.
Through the mist, a glow appears,
Bringing warmth to hidden fears.

Glistening stars like diamonds shone,
Weaving paths where light is sown.
Every twinkle tells a tale,
Radiance through the shimmering veil.

A dance of shadows, light does chase,
Painting hope with soft embrace.
In the quiet, spirits soar,
Caught in light forevermore.

Longing glimmers in our eyes,
Beneath the vast and endless skies.
With every heartbeat, every trail,
We find joy through the shimmering veil.

Dreams in the Softest Glow

In twilight's arms, we softly drift,
As dreams emerge, a tender gift.
Golden hues blend into dusk,
In the glow, our hearts we trust.

Luminous whispers, near and far,
Guide us gently like a star.
Satin skies and velvet streams,
We nestle close within our dreams.

Time pauses in a sacred space,
Where hope blooms with a gentle grace.
In the hush, the world does slow,
As we wander in the glow.

Every heartbeat, soft and light,
Cradled close this dreamy night.
As shadows lengthen and winds flow,
We find solace in the glow.

The Song of the Wandering Light

Through the forest, flickers play,
A tale of light that charts the way.
Dancing fireflies in the dark,
Each tiny spark, a vibrant mark.

Moonlit paths where silence reigns,
Guided by the softest strains.
The lull of night, a soothing sound,
The song of light where dreams abound.

Wandering whispers, gently found,
Echo through the woods profound.
Every shimmer tells a tune,
Beneath the stars, beneath the moon.

So let us follow, hand in hand,
To places where the light has spanned.
In every glow, a story bright,
We'll sing along with wandering light.

The Beauty of Forgotten Echoes

In silent woods, where shadows play,
Whispers of ghosts linger and sway.
Memories dance on a breeze so light,
Faded tales in the fall of night.

Underneath the ancient trees,
Time weaves secrets in the breeze.
Echoes of laughter from days long past,
Fleeting glances that fade so fast.

A stone table, covered in vines,
Once held feasts, now it confines.
Nature's canvas, painted in gray,
Reminds us of what slipped away.

Yet beauty rests in each soft sigh,
In echoes that never truly die.
In every shadow, a story glows,
The heart remembers what the mind knows.

Night's Haiku of Dimming Light

Stars begin to gently fade,
Moonlight whispers soft goodbyes,
Shadows stretch in twilight's haze.

Crickets sing their evening tune,
Rustling leaves in cool night air,
A world asleep, yet so aware.

Time drifts in the velvet dark,
Dreams awaken, softly sparked,
As weary eyes begin to close.

In the hush of nightly grace,
Find your peace in this embrace,
Let the dimming light unfold.

Seraphic Notes in the Lunar Air

Beneath the moon's ethereal glow,
Angelic whispers gently flow.
Melodies dance on the night's cool breath,
Notes of life, beyond even death.

Stars shimmer with a sacred light,
Guiding souls through the endless night.
Each note carries a tale untold,
Of dreams and wishes, brave and bold.

In this realm, where shadows play,
Harmony mingles with dismay.
The lunar song, a soothing balm,
Wraps the world in a peaceful calm.

Feel the magic in the air,
Seraphic whispers, light as prayer,
In every sound, a promise lies,
Beneath the watchful, ancient skies.

Festivals of Light and Shade

When dusk descends, the lanterns rise,
Joyful colors paint the skies.
In laughter's glow, we find our place,
In the dance of light, a warm embrace.

Shadows play beneath the trees,
Flickering flames and gentle breeze.
Gathered hearts and stories shared,
In this moment, we are paired.

The echoes of voices blend as one,
Underneath the setting sun.
With each heartbeat, the night unfolds,
In the warmth of tales untold.

So let the festivals commence,
In every glance, a sweet suspense.
For light and shade both have a role,
In weaving dreams that touch the soul.

A Sonnet on the Edge of Dusk

The day retreats with a tender sigh,
As shadows stretch beneath the fading light.
Embers of gold kiss the evening sky,
Painting the world in hues that feel so right.

Whispers of night dance upon the breeze,
While stars emerge, one by one, up above.
Silhouettes sway among the swaying trees,
A tranquil moment, a gift from the love.

Softly the moon casts its silver glow,
Enchanting the earth with a gentle grace.
Secrets of twilight begin to bestow,
A feeling of peace, an endless embrace.

In dusk's warm arms, all worries take flight,
For here in the stillness, we find our light.

The Shadow's Play at Twilight

As daylight fades, the shadows take their form,
They twist and bend in the waning gleam.
Figures of darkness in a subtle swarm,
Whispering softly, like a fleeting dream.

Twilight's enchantment draws them near to play,
They leap and dance in the twilight's grace.
Fleeting moments, they never may stay,
Yet linger still, casting light in their chase.

The world transforms under evening's guise,
Where laughter echoes, deep and profound.
In this dim light, the heart's joy complies,
While shadows linger, no worries surround.

As night welcomes us with its starry veil,
The shadow's dance tells a magical tale.

Echoes of Light in the Darkness

Beneath the veil of a night so deep,
The echoes of light begin to unfold.
Whispers of hope in the silence creep,
A story of dreams in the quiet told.

Through cracks of shadows, bright visions gleam,
Painting the heart with a spark of desire.
The night may shroud, but it fuels the dream,
As shadows dance in a delicate choir.

Stars twinkle softly, a guiding embrace,
Illuminating paths that are lost in the gloom.
Each flicker a sign, a celestial trace,
Reminding the spirit where beauty can bloom.

In darkness, we find the light's gentle song,
Echoes that beckon our souls to belong.

Sparkling Thoughts Beneath the Stars

Under the canvas of an endless night,
Twinkling thoughts gather, a glimmering stream.
Stars cast their magic, a mystical sight,
In the quiet moments, we dare to dream.

Each spark in the sky holds a story untold,
Adventures await in the whispers of air.
With dreams in our hearts, we gather the bold,
And chase the constellations with hope to spare.

The moon is our guide on this journey of thought,
Illuminating shadows with a soft, gentle glow.
Within this vast wonder, new wonders are sought,
As we weave our dreams into night's golden flow.

So here we shall linger, beneath the starlit dome,
With sparkling thoughts, we will always feel home.

Shadows Sing Along the Silk Road

Whispers dance on ancient trails,
Where secrets find their bliss.
Breezes weave through dusty veils,
Embracing every twist and twist.

Beneath the moon, the shadows play,
With tales of dusk in tow.
Echoes of a distant day,
As lanterns gently glow.

Silk threads shimmer in the night,
Laden with stories deep.
Winds carry dreams in flight,
While stars begin to weep.

Together they sing, a haunting song,
Of wanderers lost and found.
In the hearts where they belong,
A melody, profound.

The Tapestry of Midnight Whispers

In the tapestry of night so vast,
Whispers weave through time.
Every thread, a shadow cast,
In silence, they rhyme.

Stars embroider dreams untold,
With secrets wrapped in lace.
Midnight tales of brave and bold,
In every hidden space.

Glimmers of hope in dark's embrace,
Flickers of light entwined.
Within this quiet, sacred place,
A solace we can find.

Together we craft a tale so rare,
With soft threads of desire.
In this night, we'll share and care,
As whispers lift us higher.

Glistening Eyes and Restless Souls

In the twilight, dreams take flight,
With glistening eyes alive.
Restless souls dance in moonlight,
As shadows intertwine.

Whirling thoughts like autumn leaves,
Caught in a gentle storm.
Yearning hearts and whispered thieves,
In silence, they are warm.

Each gaze holds a thousand tales,
Of love and loss combined.
Navigating winding trails,
Where fate is often blind.

Together we'll wander, hand in hand,
Through the night's mystic maze.
With glistening eyes, we take a stand,
In a world set ablaze.

Rhapsody of Evening's Breath

Evening whispers soft and low,
As dusk begins to fall.
A rhapsody in twilight's glow,
Nature's tender call.

Stars awaken from their sleep,
Bathing us in light.
With secrets that the night will keep,
We dance in pure delight.

The moon pours silver on the sea,
A gentle lullaby.
In harmony, we take to be,
As moments drift and sigh.

Together, let our spirits rise,
In this magic that we share.
An endless dream beneath the skies,
In the evening's breath, so rare.

Luminescent Reveries

In whispers soft, the light ascends,
As dreams take flight, the night defends.
Each glow a tale, a secret spun,
Awakening hearts, as shadows run.

With starlit paths, the mind will roam,
Through echoes faint, we find our home.
In silver beams, our hopes ignite,
A dance of joy in muted light.

Beneath the moon, our stories sigh,
The past embraced, as moments fly.
In reverie, we plot the stars,
Unraveling fate, dissolving bars.

A symphony of dreams unfolds,
In luminescent whispers told.
Through night's embrace, we learn to see,
The magic spun from reverie.

An Ode to the Quiet Hour

In stillness deep, the world is bare,
As shadows breathe, and candles flare.
The clock ticks soft, its rhythm slow,
In quiet grace, the moments flow.

Whispers of thought, like gentle streams,
Guide us through the tapestry of dreams.
Each fleeting echo, an unseen prayer,
In the hush of night, we find our care.

Stars peek shyly, a celestial choir,
In the calm embrace, we build our fire.
Silent confessions danced on air,
In the quiet hour, love lays bare.

Through every sigh, the heart unfolds,
In tender solace, our spirit molds.
An ode to peace, where worries cease,
In this sacred time, we find our peace.

Twilight's Silken Harmony

As twilight drapes in silken folds,
The day softens, and night beholds.
With hues of gold, the sky ignites,
A canvas stretched where day unites.

In whispers low, the shadows weave,
A tale of warmth that we believe.
The gentle breeze, a lover's kiss,
In twilight's arms, we find our bliss.

The stars ignite as dusk descends,
In harmony where time suspends.
Each note of night, a sweet refrain,
In twilight's glow, we dance in vain.

Through every breath, the silence speaks,
A song of hearts that softly seeks.
In twilight's balm, our souls align,
Embracing dusk, where dreams entwine.

Flickers of the Nocturne's Kiss

In shadows deep, the night unfolds,
With whispers soft, a tale retold.
Flickers dance on candle's gleam,
As darkness sways, we ride the dream.

The moonlit path, where secrets dwell,
Cradles our thoughts in a silken shell.
In every blink, the stars bestow,
A kiss of light, a gentle glow.

Each heartbeat echoes, a timeless song,
In nocturne's embrace, where we belong.
With every sigh, the world withdraws,
In flickers bright, we find the cause.

As night ascends, our hopes take flight,
In dreamy realms, we chase the light.
Together lost, in twilight's bliss,
We rise anew, with the nocturne's kiss.

The Hidden Dance of Nightfall

In shadows deep, the stars emerge,
Whispers weave through the dark, a surge.
The moonlight glistens, soft and bright,
As dreams take flight in the quiet night.

Beneath the trees, the secrets sway,
With every breath, the whispers play.
The world transforms, a velvet cloak,
As night unveils the tales we spoke.

Footsteps traced on paths of time,
In rhythmic silence, hearts align.
The hidden dance of night unfolds,
In whispered stories, life retolds.

As dark entwines with glimmering light,
A tapestry of stars takes flight.
In the embrace of midnight's glance,
We find our solace in the dance.

Beneath the Expanse of Midnight

Underneath the vast, endless sky,
A symphony of nightbirds fly.
Stars like lanterns, bright and true,
Guide the dreams as they drift through.

The cool air wraps, a gentle shroud,
Beneath the moon, we sing aloud.
With every heartbeat, shadows sway,
In the stillness, night steals the day.

Crickets serenade the passing time,
Each note a echo, a soft rhyme.
The world so quiet, yet so alive,
In this stillness, our spirits thrive.

Amidst the dark, the hope does rise,
As dawn approaches, kissed by sighs.
Beneath the expanse where silence dwells,
The midnight whispers timeless spells.

Celestial Whispers on the Wind

In twilight's arms, the wind does speak,
Of ancient tales and dreams we seek.
Each breeze a hint of worlds afar,
Carrying secrets from each star.

The nightingale sings soft and low,
To the moon, a gentle glow.
In every sigh, a memory breathes,
As night unfolds its tender weaves.

Celestial whispers brush the ear,
A language only hearts can hear.
Amongst the dark, the starlight gleams,
In every shadow, the cosmos dreams.

With every gust, the night enchants,
The sky invites, and nature dances.
In the stillness, we find a thread,
Celestial whispers lead us ahead.

Moonlit Footsteps and Serene Melody

Upon the path where shadows play,
The moonlight guides our gentle sway.
Each step a note in harmony,
With nature's song, a symphony.

The trees lean in, as if to hear,
The melody that draws us near.
In silver beams, our moments weave,
A serenade we both believe.

The night unfolds, a canvas vast,
Recalling dreams both slow and fast.
With every heartbeat, love's refrain,
In moonlit footsteps, we remain.

As stars above begin to dance,
In quiet moments, souls entrance.
A serene melody in the air,
We find our peace, a world so rare.

Stars and Sighs in the Cool Air

Beneath the blanket of night,
Whispers of dreams take flight.
Cool air stirs the silent trees,
A symphony on evening's breeze.

The stars, like secrets, softly shine,
In their glow, we intertwine.
Sighs escape like fleeting thoughts,
In this moment, time forgot.

Crickets sing their gentle tune,
Beneath the watchful, silver moon.
Each blink of light, a fleeting spark,
Guiding wanderers through the dark.

In the stillness, hearts align,
Echoes of love in the divine.
As stars and sighs begin to fade,
We find the peace that dreams have made.

Undercurrents of the Night's Tranquility

The night wraps the world in calm,
Soft whispers weave a soothing psalm.
Shadows dance on silver streams,
Cradling the essence of our dreams.

Beneath the surface, secrets flow,
In the dark, their ripples grow.
Stars above in quiet splendor,
Sustain the night, they gently tender.

A rustle here, a sigh undone,
As the day fades, night has begun.
In tranquil depths, the heartbeats thrummed,\nBy nature's hand, all fears succumbed.

Within the stillness, silence speaks,
The night's embrace, our spirit seeks.
In that serene and sacred space,
We find our peace, we find our place.

Resonance of Dreaming Hearts

In the quiet where dreams reside,
Two hearts beat, side by side.
Soft echoes in the midnight hour,
Whisper tales of love's sweet power.

Each heartbeat forms a gentle song,
In the night where we belong.
With every sigh, a promise made,
In twilight's light, our fears allayed.

The stars align, they know our fate,
In their glow, we contemplate.
With every wish, the universe hears,
The resonance of our hopes and fears.

As dawn approaches, dreams take flight,
Leaving traces of the night.
Together, we weave our destinies,
In harmony with the evening breeze.

Nightfall's Caress

When shadows stretch and day does fade,
The night descends in a soft parade.
Silken breezes brush the skin,
Inviting solace to drift within.

Stars awaken in velvet skies,
Casting glimmers where silence lies.
Each twinkle, a tender embrace,
A caress of calm in this sacred space.

Moonlit pathways softly gleam,
Guiding the wanderers' quiet dream.
In the folds of darkness, we find our way,
Embracing the stillness of the drifting sway.

Through nightfall's caress, we are renewed,
As the world yawns in a tranquil mood.
In this gentle hush, we breathe and sigh,
Embraced by the moon, beneath the vast sky.

Angular Shadows

Shapes emerge in the fading light,
Angular shadows dance in flight.
Twisted forms that softly play,
In the twilight of the fading day.

Beneath the trees, a stillness grows,
Where mystery in shadows flows.
Each angle holds a whispered tale,
In twilight's grip, we set the sail.

Lost in the interplay of dusk,
An air of magic, rich and husk.
These shadows sway with secrets tight,
Guardians of the approaching night.

As darkness wraps the world in grace,
We find our rhythm, our rightful place.
In angular shadows, our spirits lift,
Carried by the night's gentle gift.

The Serengeti of Starry Eyed Dreamers

In fields of gold where dreams take flight,
The stars above, a twinkling sight.
With eyes aglow, they chase the night,
In quiet whispers, hearts ignite.

Through endless skies, their visions roam,
Each step a pulse, each breath a poem.
In serendipity, they find their home,
Among the wild, the vast unknown.

They dance with shadows, laugh with light,
Their spirits soar, their futures bright.
In every heartbeat, echoes slight,
A tapestry of dreams in flight.

Beneath the moon's soft, glowing sheen,
They weave their hopes, a joyful scene.
In this vast land, both rich and green,
The Serengeti of dreams serene.

Soft Revolutions in the Silent Night

In soft revolutions, silence reigns,
The whispers of the heart remain.
With every breath, the world refrains,
As moonlight dances on the lanes.

Stars twinkle secrets, ancient, bright,
Giving life to the gentle night.
Each moment held in soft delight,
A tranquil peace, a warm invite.

Shadows linger, but fears take flight,
In dreams wrapped close, held ever tight.
The world outside fades from our sight,
In soft revolutions, love ignites.

We find our solace, hand in hand,
In whispered words, a sacred strand.
With every heartbeat, soft and grand,
Revolutions rise, so sweetly planned.

Harmonies of the Celestial Garden

In the garden where the stars convene,
Harmonies flow—pure, serene.
With petals bright, in colors keen,
Each touch of light a vivid sheen.

The moon sings softly, a gentle guide,
While planets dance, their paths collide.
In this embrace, no fears can bide,
In celestial grace, our dreams abide.

Whispers of cosmos, the wind's sweet sighs,
In harmony's arms, the soul can rise.
Among the blooms, beneath wide skies,
The garden thrives, no need for guise.

A tapestry woven with starlit threads,
In every corner, love gently spreads.
With melodies pure, as harmony spreads,
In the celestial garden, our spirit treads.

Crystals of Light in the Quiet Gloom

In quiet gloom, crystals gleam bright,
Shimmering softly, chasing the night.
Each shard reflects a whisper of light,
Illuminating dreams, a wondrous sight.

The shadows gather, yet hope remains,
In every glimmer, joy sustains.
Through time's embrace, love still reigns,
As crystals dance on darkened plains.

With gentle warmth, they guide our way,
Through paths of twilight, night, and day.
In sparkling fragments, hearts are swayed,
Crystals of light where fears allay.

In stillness found beneath the stars,
Each luminous bead tells tales from afar.
In quiet heights, our dreams are ours,
With crystals of light, we'll raise the bar.

Serenade of Celestial Echoes

Beneath the stars, a whisper flows,
Carried by night, where soft light glows.
In the silent song, the cosmos hums,
Ancient melodies, the heart succumbs.

Galaxies twirl in a dark embrace,
Each twinkle a dream, a fleeting trace.
Time drifts gently on cosmic wings,
While the universe softly sings.

Luna's gaze holds secrets untold,
In the darkness, mysteries unfold.
Crickets chirp in harmonious tune,
As the night welcomes the silver moon.

Echoes of starlight warm the air,
Drawing us close, away from despair.
In this serenade, we find our peace,
As celestial whispers never cease.

Lullabies Under Velvet Canopies

Beneath the canopy, dreams arise,
With soft lullabies that touch the skies.
The night wraps gently, a warm embrace,
As stars peek down, a twinkling grace.

Branches sway in a rhythmic dance,
While shadows flicker, lost in a trance.
The moonlight weaves through leaves so grand,
A soothing touch from nature's hand.

Whispers of twilight float on the breeze,
Carrying secrets among the trees.
In this haven, our worries fade,
As melodies of peace serenely played.

Close your eyes, let the world drift away,
In this magic hour, let dreams stay.
Under velvet canopies, pure delight,
In lullabies, we find our light.

Shadows Dance on Midnight's Edge

On midnight's edge, shadows play,
In faded light, they drift away.
With every flutter, secrets unfold,
In the silent night, tales are told.

Moonbeams shimmer on the ground,
Whispering softly, a haunting sound.
Figures shift in the twilight glow,
As the night dance puts on a show.

Stars become witnesses of the night,
Holding each moment in shimmering light.
The chill of darkness, a shiver, a thrill,
As shadows beckon, inviting still.

In the stillness, the heart learns to roam,
Finding solace in shadows' calm home.
Midnight whispers, soft and sweet,
Where shadows dance, the lost hearts meet.

Twilight's Silken Serenade

In twilight's embrace, the day softly sighs,
As the sun dips low, painting vibrant skies.
Colors blend in a silken hue,
Crafting a serenade, old yet new.

Birds return to their hidden nests,
As silence weaves through nature's rests.
Gentle winds carry whispers so light,
In the dusk's glow, dreams take flight.

Crimson and gold, a painter's delight,
Closing the chapter on day's fading light.
In this moment, hearts breathe free,
Twilight's serenade, a cherished plea.

Stars awaken, timid and shy,
As the world transitions, night draws nigh.
In twilight's hush, time glides away,
A silken serenade at the end of the day.

Nighttime Fables of the Heart

In the hush of the starlit sky,
Whispers of dreams begin to fly.
Every shadow holds a tale,
Softly woven, like a veil.

Moonlight dances on the ground,
In its glow, sweet secrets found.
Hearts entwined beneath the night,
In the dark, all feels so right.

A gentle breeze, it calls our names,
In this stillness, love's wild flames.
Courage blooms in twilight's grace,
Here we find our sacred space.

Underneath the heavens wide,
In this fable, love won't hide.
Each heartbeat sings a quiet song,
In the night, where we belong.

Songs Cradled by the Evening Breeze

A lullaby on twilight's wing,
Echoes sweet, the nightbirds sing.
Softly swaying, shadows play,
In the dusk, they fade away.

Whispers of the cooling air,
Brings a peace, beyond compare.
Stars adorn the velvet sea,
Guiding lost souls, you and me.

The moon's embrace, a silver sight,
Wraps us gently, holds us tight.
Crickets chirp, a rhythmic dance,
Inviting hearts to take a chance.

As night unfolds her velvet arms,
We find solace in her charms.
Together here, we choose to stay,
In the songs the night does play.

Surrendering to Night's Loving Touch

As the sun dips low, we breathe,
In the twilight's glow, we weave.
Every sigh becomes a kiss,
In this moment, endless bliss.

Stars awaken, bright and clear,
Drawing close the things we fear.
In their light, we find our peace,
In the silence, doubts release.

As shadows deepen, hearts ignite,
Surrendering to the night.
Every heartbeat syncs with time,
In this darkness, love will climb.

With every breath, we shed our scars,
Underneath the loving stars.
Together, in the night we trust,
Building dreams from twilight's dust.

Whims of the Celestial Night

Captured by the moon's soft glow,
We lose ourselves in time's gentle flow.
Galaxies spin in a silent dance,
Inviting hearts to take a chance.

As constellations twinkle high,
Their stories echo through the sky.
Each flicker holds a dream so bright,
Guiding us, through the velvet night.

Mirrored in the night's embrace,
We discover our hidden grace.
With the breeze, we softly sway,
In this magic, we find our way.

So let us wander, hand in hand,
Through the night, where dreams expand.
In the whims of stars, we'll trust,
For in the night, there's only us.

Illumination in the Depths of Serenity

In quiet pools where shadows lay,
A gentle light finds its own way.
Ripples dance on the surface calm,
Cradled in nature's soothing balm.

Beneath the stars in twilight's embrace,
Dreams whisper softly, leaving no trace.
Each moment held in a timeless flow,
A peace discovered within the glow.

With every breath, the stillness sings,
Carrying secrets of simple things.
The heart listens, the mind takes flight,
In the depths of serene, endless night.

Glimmers of hope twinkle afar,
Guiding lost souls like a bright star.
In illumination's soft caress,
Peace blooms, a bright, loving kindness.

Requiem of the Hidden Glow

In shadows cast by a dusky light,
Lies a tale of the hidden night.
Whispers echo through the deep,
Where wishes awaken from their sleep.

A melody drifts on the softest breeze,
Carrying dreams that put the heart at ease.
In the silence, a spirit takes flight,
Illuminated by a spark of night.

Each flicker hints at what might be,
The unseen pathways that set us free.
A requiem sung with a gentle sigh,
For the lost and the loved who quietly lie.

In the depths of the dark, a glow resides,
Guiding the souls through unseen tides.
A symphony woven with threads of fate,
In the hidden light, we celebrate.

A Canvas of Silent Whispers

On a canvas painted in twilight hues,
Silent whispers share tender views.
Colors blend, emotions collide,
Artistry flourished where hearts confide.

Brush strokes dance with delicate grace,
Capturing moments, time's sweet embrace.
Each whisper a note from within the soul,
Creating a masterpiece that makes us whole.

Underneath the stars, stories unfold,
In the quiet night, secrets are told.
A canvas alive with dreams and desires,
Fanned by the breath of creative fires.

In the silence, inspiration flows,
Like a river where the true heart grows.
A tapestry woven with hope, love, and light,
In the beauty of whispers, we find our sight.

Tales Woven Underneath the Night Sky

Underneath the vast, starlit dome,
Tales are spun that feel like home.
Each star a word, each moonbeam a line,
Crafting stories that in silence shine.

The night sky wraps us in its embrace,
A canvas where dreams find their place.
Magic dawns as shadows take flight,
In whispered tales shared by the night.

Hearts conspire with the gentle breeze,
As secrets dance among the trees.
With every breath, a story is told,
In the tapestry of dark, bright, and bold.

Woven together, our voices unite,
Creating legends in the stillness of night.
Underneath the celestial glow so high,
We celebrate life with each heartfelt sigh.

A Symphony of Distant Glows

In twilight's embrace, the shadows play,
Notes of gold drift, fading away.
Each flicker tells tales of worlds afar,
Guided by the light of a distant star.

Winds whisper softly through the night,
Inviting dreams to take their flight.
An echo of music, sweet and low,
A symphony sung by the softest glow.

Colors entwined in the velvet sky,
As dark meets light, they dance and fly.
Melodies linger in the evening air,
Carried by starlight, free of care.

Each note a promise, a silent vow,
To chase away all sorrow now.
In this celestial concert, hearts ignite,
A symphony of dreams in the cool, clear night.

Nightsong in the Whispering Trees

Beneath the canopy where secrets dwell,
The trees weave songs, a timeless spell.
Leaves flutter softly, a gentle cheer,
Cradling stories only night can hear.

Moonlight spills gold on the mossy floor,
An ancient chorus; listen, implore.
The wind carries whispers from branch to bark,
Notes of the night, alive in the dark.

Crickets are strumming their midnight tune,
A serenade kissed by silver moon.
Echoes of laughter from long ago,
In the heart of the woods, where shadows grow.

Every rustle, a word unspoken,
In the dark, the silence is broken.
Nature's orchestra sways and swirls,
A nightsong sung by the whispering worlds.

Stars Weaving Tales of Slumber

In the quiet dusk, the stars appear,
Weaving dreams like silk, crystal clear.
Tales of wonder, of hope and flight,
Spun in the fabric of the night.

Constellations connect in glowing threads,
Telling stories of the lost and the led.
A tapestry rich with myth and lore,
Each twinkle a secret, forevermore.

As eyelids flutter and worries cease,
The night embraces with tender peace.
Stars blink softly, in rhythmic dance,
Inviting the weary to take a chance.

In slumber's grip, wanderers soar,
Through galaxies opened, forever explore.
Weaving a future where dreams ignite,
Under the gaze of that shimmering light.

Whispers of the Starlit Sky

The night sky sighs with whispers divine,
Secrets of ages in every line.
Celestial voices drift through the dark,
A lullaby sung by each glowing spark.

Stars beckon softly, their tales unfold,
Of journeys taken, of brave and bold.
In the hush of night, a promise flows,
In dreams we dance where the stardust glows.

Galaxies twirl in a shimmering waltz,
While the universe watches, it never halts.
A canvas of wishes, of fears set free,
In the heart of the night, just you and me.

So close your eyes and let thoughts stray,
To the whispers of worlds where wishes play.
In the starlit grace, find your peace,
As the night carries on, and whispers cease.

Chants of the Starlit Depths

In shadows deep, the whispers call,
The night unfolds, embracing all.
Beneath the veil, the secrets lie,
As moonlight drips from velvet sky.

With gentle grace, the echoes sing,
Of distant worlds and forgotten things.
A cosmic hymn, a silken thread,
Binding the lost, the dreams once tread.

The stars ignite with ancient fire,
Each flicker sparks a deep desire.
The night, a canvas, vast and wide,
Where wishes dance and hopes reside.

Among the deep, the spirits weave,
A tale of love we all believe.
As starlit chants fill the night air,
We stand enchanted, free of care.

The Whispered Secrets of a Bright Glimmer

A glimmer bright, a tale untold,
In whispered secrets, the stars unfold.
Each twinkle holds a story sweet,
Of journeys long, where hearts dare meet.

In twilight's glow, the shadows play,
As dreams emerge in soft array.
With every breath, a spark ignites,
The cosmos weaves its wondrous sights.

The nightingale sings, a soothing song,
Where all the brave and bold belong.
With open hearts, we yearn and strive,
For glimmers bright, we feel alive.

In distant realms, where wishes flow,
The secrets whisper, and love will grow.
Under the stars, we find our way,
In every glimmer, hope holds sway.

Twilight Invitations and Celestial Flights

Twilight beckons with open arms,
Inviting dreams and hidden charms.
As stars appear with gentle grace,
We find our joy in this sacred space.

Celestial flights through endless night,
We soar on whispers, hearts in flight.
With every moment, time stands still,
As cosmic wonders our spirits fill.

The horizon blushes with hues divine,
Each breath we take, a sacred sign.
In twilight's glow, we lose our fear,
Embracing all that brings us near.

Together we share this journey bright,
In the dance of shadows, in the light.
Hand in hand, we rise above,
In twilight's arms, we find our love.

The Enigmatic Dance of Stars

The stars align, a dance begins,
In rhythms deep, our heartache thins.
Each twirl and spin, a cosmic rhymes,
Unraveling tales across the times.

With gravity's pull, they glide and play,
Lost in the night, they drift away.
An enigmatic ballet unfolds,
Of hopes and dreams the universe holds.

Beneath the night, our spirits sway,
Caught in the magic of their array.
Each twinkling light, a guide from afar,
In the quiet whispers of a shooting star.

Through realms unseen, the dance continues,
Where love is forged and hope renews.
In the arc of night, we learn to trust,
In the dance of stars, together we must.

Starlit Serenades Among the Pines

Underneath the vast, dark sky,
Whispers of the night wind sigh.
Stars like jewels flicker bright,
In the pines, a soft delight.

Crickets sing their gentle tune,
Moonlight bathes the woods in bloom.
Echoes dance on evening's breath,
Cradled in the arms of earth.

Branches sway with sweet allure,
Nature's heart beats soft and pure.
Lost in tales of time and space,
Finding peace in this embrace.

Silhouettes in shadows play,
Memories drift, then fade away.
Starlit serenades reveal,
The magic that the night can steal.

Echoing Through the Quietude

Silence wraps the world in calm,
Whispers rise like morning balm.
Nature's breath, a gentle sigh,
Echoes dance where dreams can fly.

Footsteps soft on dew-kissed ground,
Voices lost, yet all around.
Time slows down, the heart can hear,
Every sound, both far and near.

In the stillness, thoughts take flight,
Floating softly in the night.
Every echo finds its way,
To the dawn of a new day.

In the quiet, secrets dwell,
Stories whispered, tales to tell.
Echoing through nature's creed,
In the silence, we are freed.

Embrace of the Whispering Shadows

When the sun begins to fade,
Shadows stretch in evening's shade.
Whispers linger in the air,
Secrets hidden everywhere.

Branches weave a tangled song,
As the night draws ever long.
In the dark, we find our way,
Guided by the stars that play.

Embrace the hush where spirits roam,
Find in shadows a quiet home.
The night unfolds with tender grace,
Weaving dreams in soft embrace.

In each rustle, hear a call,
As the world begins to fall.
In the quiet, night unfolds,
Stories whispered, old yet bold.

Celestial Chimes of Serenity

In the night, a gentle sound,
Celestial chimes all around.
Tinkling soft like bells in dreams,
Floating on the moonlit beams.

Stars align in harmony,
Singing notes of reverie.
Cosmic wishes start to bloom,
As the heavens fill the room.

Muffled echoes drift afar,
Touched by light of every star.
Whispers thread through time and space,
Embracing night's warm, sweet grace.

In this melody we find,
A peace that soothes the restless mind.
Celestial chimes of bliss unite,
Guiding souls to rest tonight.

Milton Keynes UK
Ingram Content Group UK Ltd.
UKHW021928011224
451790UK00005B/59